ANTHOLOGY OF POETRY
BY
YOUNG AMERICANS®

2000 EDITION
VOLUME XCIV

Published by Anthology of Poetry, Inc.

©*Anthology of Poetry by Young Americans*®
2000 Edition
Volume XCIV
All Rights Reserved©

Printed in the United States of America

To submit poems
for consideration in the year 2001 edition of the
Anthology of Poetry by Young Americans®,
send to: poetry@asheboro.com or

> Anthology of Poetry, Inc.
> PO Box 698
> Asheboro, NC 27204-0698

Authors responsible
for originality of poems submitted.

The Anthology of Poetry, Inc.
307 East Salisbury • P.O. Box 698
Asheboro, NC   27204-0698

Paperback ISBN: 1-883931-25-8
Hardback ISBN: 1-883931-26-6

Anthology of Poetry by Young Americans®
is a registered trademark of
Anthology of Poetry, Inc.

As the new century dawns, the 2000 edition of the *Anthology of Poetry by Young Americans*® provides the fresh slate for the young minds that have shared thought and perspective with us over the past eleven years. In that time, we have witnessed the colorful expansion of the fabric of life, woven ever more brilliantly by poignant thought transferred to words, from the observant young people who have participated. It is through the senses of the young that we retain our youth, our optimism, and our curiosity. The eyes of our young have brought to our books vivid imagery; some as fine as a master impressionist, and others as frightening as the darkest storyteller. Their ears have played music for us page after page. Our children's sense of smell has sent us time traveling to the past, to some of our earliest memories. These young poets, through the sense of touch have reminded us of the softest, safest feelings that our hands can remember. And from their young tongues, that have tasted for the first time the sweetness and bitterness of the small moments of life, we can savor the flavors of youth. The words and wisdom of these young poets have provided a collection of roadmaps for life. Just when we think we know the way, a small but accurate path is charted and handed to us by one of our children. It is to all of these poets that we owe the debt of thanks. We are expecting great things from them in the future.

The Editors

FRIENDSHIPS

Always watch for me,
Let me soak in your light,

Keep me on a straight road,
I'll soon be in the right.

Where I am right now isn't true,
Of this I am sure,

Please stand by me,
I will soon be pure.

Stay with me,
I'll be fine,

The right road will be here,
Only in its own time.

I need your help,
The protection from the world,

I will be with you,
At your side,
Peacefully curled.

All your guidance will help me through,
If you ever need me,
I'll come running to you.

Rebecca Bradley
Age: 13

Fall is when
Leaves are falling,
Flowers are dying,
Days are getting shorter,
Squirrels are collecting nuts,
And birds are flying south.

Nicholas Pflanz
Age: 8

Fall is when
leaves are changing color
leaves are falling
animals are getting food
birds are flying
and flowers are dying

Aaron Fluehr
Age: 8

FALL

Fall is Thanksgivingtime,
and we have Halloween.
Some people are ghosts.
Fall smells like animals,
pumpkin pie baking in the oven,
hot chocolate warming
in the microwave.
It tastes like yummy turkey
on Thanksgiving.
I like to eat mashed potatoes
and apple pie.
Fall sounds like rabbits nibbling grass,
and squirrels climbing trees.
It reminds me of baking cookies
in the oven,
roaring winds,
and deer walking through the leaves.
Fall makes me feel
like the happiest person in my family,
and I feel special.

                                        Alyssa Loch
                                        Age: 8

SPRING

Spring is warm.
Animals have babies.
Cows give us milk.
Bees give us honey.
Spring smells like roses
and pumpkin pie.
It tastes like chicken soup.
It sounds like birds singing.
It reminds me of dogs,
cats, and ducks.
Spring makes me feel good
playing in the grass.
My family likes spring, too!

Casey Jones
Age: 8

WINTER

Winter is the time of year when snow falls.
It smells like fresh air and fire smoke.
It tastes like ice, candy, and soup.
It sounds like wind and people yelling,
"It's cold! It's cold!"
It reminds me of the freezer.
Winter makes me feel very cold.

Ashlea Krumm
Age: 8

QUESTIONS

I have so many questions to ask.
But I don't know how to ask them.
I don't know when to ask them.
I don't know who to ask...
Or why I even have so many questions.

Then I realized,
I knew how to ask them.
I knew when to ask them.
I knew why I had so many questions...
It's God.

Amber Lynn Lovins
Age: 14

The world is turning into fall,
turning from hot to cold
turning from a lot of leaves
to not very many leaves
turning from not very foggy to foggy
turning from fun to boring
It's fall.

Alexis M. Ziegelmeier
Age: 8

THE GUY

The guy,
he ran.
He ran with all his might.
The guy, fell down,
he fell down with a fright.
The guy,
got up.
He got up with a stumble,
the guy, said ow.
He said it with a grumble.

Derek Schatzman
Age: 13

MY PUPPY

My puppy is two
he is as sweet as can be.

His name is Wally,
he is a smally.

He only bites your toes
but not a lot no, no, no
but I love him so yes, yes, yes!

Lissa Amin
Age: 8

I soared through the air
With the greatest of ease
I flew through the air
As fast as I possibly could
Above the cities, people, and trees
I curved to the left
I curved to the right
BUMP!!
Ouch, I fell out of bed!

Heather Scholl

SOMEDAY

Someday I'll wake up
And someone big and mighty
My hero
Sitting at the foot of my bed
Hoping for me to get up
And give him a kiss
He'll say
Wake up sunshine
As the sun creeps
Through my closed shades
And then when I open my eyes
I find him
My hero
My dad

Stephanie Roewer

WHY?

I have one question and one question only: Why?

Why do we live?
Why do we wake up every morning?
Why do we go to sleep every night?

Why do we have crushes?
Why do we fall in love?
Why do we have kids?

Why are we afraid to explore the millennium?
Why don't we want to live in the future?

Instead of walking with our heads down
And fearing the future,
Why don't we walk with our heads high,
And imagine and explore the future?

Rebecca Hopper

LOVE

Together forever
Never apart
Kind and sharing
Like a big heart

Suzanne Rayle

SCHOOL

School is pretty rough at first
Once you get the hang of it
It's not the worst.
But when it's the end of the year
You're full of joy and laughter
You spend the summer playing
Then come back to school
For tutoring and after-school detentions
That's the laughter that comes from teachers
That's the disaster

Amanda Laing

FALLEN ANGEL

Down to earth
Feet on the ground
Look straight ahead
Please don't turn around
In all I do
I'm here for you
I'm your fallen angel

Kandace Clark

LIVING

I look back upon my life,
You see I strive to survive.
Dying isn't easy,
But living does seem hard.
Some folks don't care if they die...
They just want to leave a mark.
When people try to live,
I think it's just too hard.
But maybe what they call living,
Really isn't worth to start.

But if living isn't all, that it's shot up to be,
I'll forgive you, but others won't you see.
So I'll let you go, play and shout.
I think I'll just watch... and sit this one out.

I guess I can't make you understand.
Not on anyone I don't put a blame.
But maybe when we're dead and gone,
You'll see another generation and feel the same.

I write and write although it does no good.
I can't change the world...
But maybe someday I'll at least be understood.
Since doing drugs and giving up
Will never help much,
I suggest you let go of this awful grudge.

Levi Florence
Age: 13

COLOR

What is pink?
A flower is pink
by a waterfall

What is red?
A car is red
when it is outside
and a new car that goes fast

What is blue?
A cover is blue
where people put their books in

What is white?
A calendar is white
by the door in Mrs. Taubert's class

What is yellow?
A chair is yellow
by a desk where Jessica Harr sits

What is green?
The grass is green
with the bugs and flowers

What is orange?
An orange is orange
and an orange is sweet

Clayton Sapp
Age: 9

COLOR

What is brown?
A tree is brown
Trees are my friends, on hot, hot, summer days
I love the shade they give to me

What is green?
Grass is green
I am thankful for the grass because I can sit down
And have a picnic on the nice, soft, cool grass

What is red?
A rose is red
They are soft and smell so sweet
And I love to put them on my head

What is yellow?
A sun is yellow
It makes the warmth of the day in the summer
And makes me feel all mellow

What is blue?
A butterfly is blue
A little blue butterfly floating through the air
Like a small piece of paper
Going to I don't know where

What is orange?
A pumpkin is orange
A pumpkin glows in the dark
With an ugly, scary face looking at me

What is white?
A cloud is white
A little white cloud as puffy as can be
But it is very cushiony as you can see

What is black?
A spider is black
Very scary after Halloween

What is purple?
A tulip is purple
Very soft, very smooth
But really pretty too.

What is pink?
A sunset is pink
I like the sight of the pink sunset
But it soon will be night
And the sun will be gone in a wink of an eye

> Lindsay Miser
> Age: 8

COLOR

What is pink?
Folders are pink
Where I keep my papers.

What is red?
A shirt is red
A fuzzy furry shirt

What is blue?
The sky is blue
Where the sun can come up

What is white?
A table is white
You can put your food on it

What is yellow?
A piece of paper is yellow
You can draw and write

What is green?
A book is green
With a cover that is pretty

What is orange?
A marker is orange
And you can color with it.

Ashley Hill
Age: 8

COLOR

What is pink?
A curtain is pink
By a bathroom sink

What is red?
An ant is red
In its hole

What is blue?
The sky is blue
Where the people and birds fly

What is white?
The clouds are white
In the white sky

What is yellow?
A daisy is yellow
Like Maisy the mouse

What is green?
A weed is green
With a stem

What is orange?
A flag is orange
On its pole

Brandon Higgins
Age: 8

THE RAINBOW

R -- Jesus will reign forever
A -- All to him will bow
I -- I love him most of all
N -- Now is the time to ask him in
B -- Bring all your cares to him
O -- Open up your heart to him
W -- Witness your love for him

Keisha Gyarmati
Age: 11

CAR RIDE

Please excuse my handwriting,
I guess it's hard to read.
I want this poem to be perfect,
I'll tell you what I need.

I need a car that rides smooth,
doesn't wobble from side to side.
I guess you can probably tell,
I'm really on a car ride.

Sarah A. Blanton

WINTER

Cold, crisp, chilly, days,
Jackets, sweaters, jeans, coats, hats,
Trying to keep warm.

David Newberry
Age: 11

THE BIBLE

The Bible is a book of stories
Songs of many glories
There's Adam and Eve and dogs that bark
Noah and his family who built the ark
It tells of kings and queens
Of shepherds and giants and all those things
It says to worship God and nothing else
To love our neighbor as ourselves
How the baby Jesus was born in a manger
And how Herod put him in great danger
It shows us love and kindness, peace and grace
And how Daniel in the lions' den had great faith
It tells how Jesus died on the cross for you and me
And if we except him we can go to Heaven you see?
It says there's going to be a great rapture
And that the unsaved people will be captured
If we don't rely on Jesus we can't have eternal life
So the most important is that we receive Christ

Jerusha Miller
Age: 12

THE DECISION

Two years is what they took
I can't change that
because society shows no love for a crook.
Trapped inside this cage
sometimes losing my mind
Thinking about my grandparents.
My girl and all this time
It's so hard
I'm not counting months I'm counting years
Reminisce on yesterday and my eyes fill with tears
Like 2-PAC said,
"Even them thugs gotta cry."
I'm a prime example 2-PAC wasn't telling a lie
So day after day and night after night
I pray to the Lord because he'll make it all right
When I get out I'm going to try to make a change
It's going to be hard
because the street life revolves around
the (Dope Game)
This dope game life isn't to be messed with,
you either end up dead or locked in the pen.
Where society talks about you
like you're nothing
they say your life has come to an end.
So please just open your eyes
and see what I'm tryin' to preach
To the young players' hearts
is where I'm tryin' to reach
Take it from us older soldiers
who's done been through all of this
Satan uses the dope game to get to you
so you better not slip

It will take your family
it will take your possessions.
So you better change for the good
and make a confession
Because if not you'll be writing your own poem
locked in a cell
Then you'll end up spending eternal life
burning in Hell.
Growing up with those friends
I got my rep as a thief
I told myself I wouldn't get caught
I thought I was unique
Drinkin' and smokin' with my friends
and roaming the streets
Hittin' hundred of licks messin' with freaks
I really didn't care I thought I couldn't be stopped
Until I saw Judge Wyler's gavel drop.
Two years the maximum sentence
that's what she gave me
I looked at my grandmother,
she was crying, saying
"please don't take my baby."
So now I'm at the bottom
and I've got to work at the top.
At first I prayed and said,
"God please make this dope game stop."
But now I realize that it is a prayer hard to answer
because the dope game is a predator
like the Carolina Panthers.
Now I must become a man
and make a change on my own
In here is the only beginning,
the real struggle is at home
Satan is out there

and he is ready to seek my blood.
Sorry, Satan, I've got a new partner
now I'm rollin' with the man above
So to all ya'll players out there
who think you can't make that change
You just heard my story
my name is Jeff Reed,
and now I'm out of the dope game.

Jeffrey Reed

The world is turning into fall.
   turning from summer to fall.
turning from summer to autumn.
   turning from hot to cold.
turning from vacation to school.
   It's fall.

Angelee Donders
Age: 8

BARBARIANS, VILLAINS, AND WOMEN, OH MY!

A bnormal
B arbarians
C atch
D ogs
E ating
F ingernailed
G oats.

H andsome
I mposters
J ump
K nife-throwing
L adies
M aking
N otes
O f
P ackaged
Q uaker
R ations.

S oon
T hey
U nraveled
V illains
W hile
X -raying
Y oung
Z ebras.

Dustin Cory Harless
Age: 12

I WISH

I wish I could remember
 what it was like being born.
I'd like to remember
 all the books I've torn.
I wish I could remember
 my house long ago.
I wish I could remember
 the garden I'd hoe.
I wish I could remember
 my first day at school.
I wish I could remember
 the sweater of wool.
I wish I could remember
 my long-lost friends.
I wish I could remember
 how to stretch and bend.
I wish I could remember
 the first book I've read.
I wish I could remember
 not to lose my head.
I wish I could remember
 my first pet.
I wish I could remember
 to bring my fishing net.
I wish that I could remember
 all that was forgotten.
Until that day
 I shall lay
and dream of all the lost memories.

Miranda Lovins
Age: 14

ANGEL

She was here but now she's gone
We didn't get to say so long
But now she's in a better place
Showing off her pretty face
So beautiful even the angels cry
Maybe she's an angel in disguise
But for so long she blessed us
With her joyful, cheery, kindness
We must remember what she gave
And know that's what we must save
She didn't get to graduate or have her last dance
But up there she surely will get her second chance.

Sarah Kay Bullock
Age: 13

MY FAVORITE FOOD

P izza tastes very good!
   Just the way it should!
I like ice cream too!
   When I get a headache I say Wahoo!
E ggs are my favorite breakfast for real!
   It's a very good meal!

Matthew F. Voto
Age: 8

COLOR

What is pink?
A color is pink
by a pretty river

What is red?
An apple is red
in its apple tree

What is blue?
The ocean is blue
where the sun is

What is white?
A cloud is white
in the sky at night

What is yellow?
Sand is yellow
blowing in the wind

What is green?
Grass is green
by a waterfall

What is orange?
The sunset is orange
in the pretty sky

Jessica Houze
Age: 10

COLOR

What is pink?
A flower is pink
By the kitchen sink

What is red?
A rose is red
In its vase by the bathroom sink

What is blue?
The sky is blue
Where the prairies lay

What is white?
White is a cat
Running through the wind

What is yellow?
Yellow is a dog
Playing in the field

What is green?
The meadow is green
With flowers so pretty

What is orange?
A fox is orange
Oranger than oranges

Jessica N. Harr
Age: 8

BRUSH STROKES

I am from faded blue jeans,
  From Farmall and Pioneer.
I am from the dirt in the tobacco field
  (fresh, old, full of hard work.)
I am from sunflower seeds,
  the walnut tree whose leaves
    I raked so carefully
      as if they were my own children.
I am from hard work and brown eyes,
  from Dave and Trina Stutz.
I am from the outspoken
and do-it yourselfers,
    from, "If you do it yourself and work hard,
      then you only have yourself to thank."
I am from " ... the Lord is my Shepherd,
I shall not want,"
  and the Our Father that I learned at church.
I am from Ohio and Germany,
  mashed potatoes and green beans,
    from the quilt my mamaw gave to me
  when I was five,
    and the tractor my father pretended
    to let me drive in from the field.
In the cedar chest at my grandmother's house,
  lies my soul
    along with painted memories of my childhood.

Holly Stutz
Age: 14

LOVE IS LOVE

I am nothing special,
  of this I am sure.
I am a common girl,
  with common thoughts,
    and so far I've led a common life.
There are no monuments dedicated to me,
  and my name will soon be forgotten,
    but I've loved another with all my heart
      and soul
        and to me, this is enough.

Tara Ninichuck
Age: 13

SPRING

Spring is when flowers come out.
Spring is Eastertime.
Spring is time to play and run.
Spring is my birthday.
It smells like pretty flowers.
It tastes like big, red apples.
It sounds like birds chirping.
It reminds me of when I found a bird.
Spring makes me feel happy.

Kelsey Humbert
Age: 8

WHERE I'M FROM

I am from peanut butter and jelly sandwiches
from JIF and Welch's
I am from boards on a deck
(painted, decorated, smelling fresh)
I am from fields, lilacs, and trees
The fields stretched to the woods

I am from whiffle ball and church activities
From Regina and Dave
I'm from the Gilkison's and the Kaylor's
From keep trying and great work

I'm from Sunday school, Gleaner's,
and memorizing the books of the Bible
I'm from the Jewish Hospital and North Street
Scrambled eggs and bacon
From my grandpa's tractor wreck
and his hospital bed
the Corvette stories he always told

In the drawer
Stacked picture upon picture
Some distant memories
Friends and families from everywhere

Zachary Gilkison
Age: 12

BABY-SITTING

I taught my sister to pinch,
    to stick out her tongue,
        to make funny noises,
to do a handstand,
    to stand up in the shopping cart,
to play peek-a-boo,
    to run, not walk,
        to take her own dirty diapers to the trash,
    to never listen to Mom,
to get everything she wants,
    to go to the highchair when she is hungry,
and to tear up the diapers she doesn't like...
... and my sister is only one year old.

Annette Jones

FALL

Fall is cold.
It smells like leaves, soup,
and pumpkin pie.
It tastes like apples.
It sounds like the crunching of red leaves.
It reminds me of my birthday.
Fall makes me feel like raking leaves.

Brittany King
Age: 9

FLOWER

I am a flower.
I wonder what it would be like to be a person.
I hear people laugh at me because I'm short.
I want to know when I will be big
Like the other flowers
I am a flower.

I pretend to be a human
I feel the wind go by
I touch my neighbor Rose
And ask her some questions about being big
I worry about being picked
I cry at night because I am lonely
I am a flower

I understand that nobody wants me
I say to myself it will be okay
I dream of being one of the Roses
I try not to cry after my dream
I hope to grow up and be big
Like the other flowers
I am a flower.

Valeri Day
Age: 12

ENERGETIC ANIMALS

A ttentive
 B utterflies
  C rown
   D owny
    E lectric
     F rames.

G reen
 H amsters
  I ntercepted
   J ellied
    K issers.

L ovely
 M ice
  N ever
   O ccupied
    P retty
     Q uick
      R ats.

S aber
 T oothed
  U ndertake
   V icious
    W oodpeckers
     X -ray
      Y ams to a
       Z oo.

Austen Leigh Bandy
Age: 11

SPECIAL GUESTS

Halloween parties
Inviting Frankenstein's friends
Scary ghost stories

Timothy Menshouse
Age: 11

FROG

Frog, frog sat on a log.
Frog, frog here comes a dog.
Frog, frog sees a fly.
Gulp! What a tasty treat in the sky!

Spenser Rahm
Age: 8

NATURE

Kids playing in woods
Kids playing with insects, bugs, snakes
Kids playing in leaves.

Jade Walker
Age: 11

My pumpkin played a game,
And I don't think it's very lame.
She has a friend named Boo,
But she has goo.
My pumpkin wore a hat,
And for lunch she ate a bat.

Katie Lynn Barthel

THINGS I AM

I am smart and friendly.
I wonder if the world is coming to an end.
I hear water splashing.
I want to live forever.
I am smart and friendly.

I pretend to like school.
I feel sad about homeless people.
I touch my puppy's fur.
I worry about my grades in school.
I cry when I think of people dying.
I am smart and friendly.

I understand that I can't have everything I want.
I say that there is a god.
I dream of being famous.
I try to be a good child.
I hope that I'll go to Heaven.
I am smart and friendly.

> Brittany L. Spradling
> Age: 12

WINTER

Winter comes every year,
So swift so fast no one can hear.
In its clouds is something white,
When it falls it is a wonderful sight.
Winter will sometimes bring the occasional ice,
But when the sun rises it shines so nice.
Winter will bring a cold crisp air,
That in time will make the trees go bare.
Winter will bring snow that will cause school delays,
But soon all that snow will melt away.

Brian Patrick Schumacher
Age: 12

THEN AND NOW

I used to listen to pop rock music,
   But now I listen to a heavy metal,
      Head-bangin' kind of music.
I used to wear normal clothes
Like plain blue jeans and shirts,
   But now I wear skater clothes.
I used to be afraid to fly in a plane or a jet,
   But now that's all I want to do.
I used to not have any pets,
   But now I have a dog named Shiloh.

Chris Smith
Age: 14

Charlie
Funny, athletic, golfer, blond hair,
Lover of golf, soccer, money.
Who needs family, friends, freetime,
Basketball, golf, soccer.
Who fears big hairy spiders
Very very high up with no support.
Who gives positive attitude, smile, respect.
Resident of Ohio.
I would like to see me living in Oregon.
McLelland

>Charlie McLelland
>Age: 10

WINTER WEATHER

Winter is cold
I make snowballs out of snow
Ice is fun to throw

>Nathan Jones
>Age: 11

AT NIGHT

The stars at night are bright,
The moon at night has special light to guide you.
The night is dark while the other side
of the earth has light.
At night bats fly by and creatures come out.
At night while you're in bed
you have dreams in your head,
about monsters and other fun stuff,
while you're asleep on your pillow
that's made out of fluff.
And at night remember look at the moon
and it will guide you through the night
with its special light.

Cara Lucke
Age: 8

Pumpkin
round, fat
still, quiet, relaxed
being harvested
Pumpkin

Johnny Charles
Age: 9

WINTER

I like throwing snowballs
But I hate when it hits other people's snow walls
I think it's fun to play in the snow when it falls
I like making angels out of snow
But I don't like when the snow blows
Because then it wrecks my snow angel
And it puts them in an angle.

Adam Jessen
Age: 9

Cider
wet, juicy
wiggles, jiggles, moves
good, tasty
Delicious!!!!

Brittany Kenyon
Age: 8

WINTERS

Winters are cold
Winters are bold
Winters are fun
Especially in the sun

> Morgan Di Silvestro
> Age: 8

Monarch
colors, beautiful
flies, eats nectar
hurrying fast
Monarch

> Bradley Salunek
> Age: 8

LOVE

Love is the color of red with passion
It sounds like the beating of a throbbing heart
for the one person they adore
It taste like sweet chocolate
on a hot sunny day
Love smells of a fresh cut rose
Looks as cute as a sweet puppy
Love's addicting and leaves you feeling confused
and touched by the feeling

Kimberly Ann Haines
Age: 13

ALL HUMAN

We are all human.
Some of us like to play.
Some of us like to sing.
Some of us like to read.
Some of us like to write.
Some of us like to collect.
Some of us like to draw.
Some of us like to do math.
We all like so many different things
but we are all human.

Kristen Coburn
Age: 8

HORSES, HORSES, HORSES

Horses eat hay all day.
My horse's name is Freckles.
She has lots of speckles!
Freckles is gray and loves to play.
Freckles likes to have fun and run.
Horses love to have fun in the sun.
They love to nuzzle with their muzzle.
Freckles jumps the creek
without getting weak.
Freckles eats her favorite treats.
Freckles stands under trees
to catch a cool breeze.
I'll be her friend
until the very end.

Sarah Thomas
Age: 8

LEAVES

Leaves are always falling to the ground
  They do this without making a sound.
Leaves fall off trees.
  In the gentle breeze.
Leaves are seen.
  The colors of red, orange, and green.

Christina Gilene
Age: 8

CHRISTMAS TREES

When you buy a Christmas tree
you have to get a good one.
They weigh a ton!

There are several different types.
All grow in the sun.
Picking your tree is so much fun!

Sarah Williams
Age: 9

SHOES

There are shoes for wishing
   and shoes for mud squishing.
There are shoes to wear when you have the blues
   or shoes to wear when you cruise.
You can wear shoes when doing flips
   Some shoes even have zips.
I keep my shoes behind the door
   You can open and find several more.
Shoes are placed on your bare feet
   So you don't get hurt when on the street.

Christina Jackson
Age: 8

SUMMER

My family has a swimming pool.
   It is heated by fuel.
Summer is a time to play.
   I really hope it can stay.
In the summer ducks quack.
   I hear them when my belly makes a smack!
I hope the summer can stay.
   So I have more time to play!

Riley Bagnall
Age: 8

FUN ON A LOG

Jumping on a log is fun
   Just like eating a hamburger on a bun
Sitting on a log is nice
   Especially when watching mice
I like to play on my log
   In the early morning fog

Steven Hilton
Age: 9

BROTHERS

Brothers are mean
Brothers are nice
But you're in-between
And that's what I like

                                  Lisa Cobb
                                  Age: 13

Rabbit
soft, furry
hops, eats, cuddles
happy, perky, glad creature
Animal

                              Candice Metcalf
                              Age: 8

AUTUMN

Autumn smells
like the wonderful smell of nature.
Autumn sounds
like wonderful never-ending music.
Autumn looks
like the best picture ever created.
Autumn feels
like twenty baby kittens rubbing against you.
Autumn tastes
like the best pear of them all.

Daniel Lawson Sturgill
Age: 9

SUMMER

Summer is hot.
It is green grass.
It smells like chocolate.
It tastes like cookies.
It sounds like birds chirping.
It reminds me of when I got tackled
at football practice.
Summer makes me feel good
because I go swimming.

Bradley Lloyd
Age: 9

My pumpkin is really mad,
But that doesn't mean he is sad.
Pumpkins are very cool,
But they do not rule.
They carved my pumpkin last night,
But that is all right.

Alex Chilelli
Age: 8

Raking leaves
fun, easy
falling, drying, hanging
high, jump
Raking leaves

Andy Miller Jr.
Age: 8

My pumpkin is fat,
Her friend is a bat.
She lives in LA,
And doesn't like to play.
Pumpkin Patch is so pretty,
But needs to lose weight, what a pity!

Sarah Bethany Craycraft
Age: 9

Friends
playful, fun
jump, run, skip
happy, glad, joyful, pleasant
Schoolmates

Rebecca Callahan
Age: 8

Rippity rat, my pumpkin was a brat,
So I hit him with a bat.
It made him have a hole on his top,
It went KABOOM POP!
It is orange and wears a cap.
Its brain is like a map.

Sarah Luti
Age: 9

Wind
north, moving
blowing, cool, compelling
gusty breeze, cold, brisk
Gale

Ben Gallenstein
Age: 9

FLOWERS

A person that likes flowers,
Will have different types of powers.
My favorite flower is a daisy.
My Aunt Teresa is half crazy.
I don't like a marigold,
I think they smell like mold.

                                  Megan Wright
                                       Age: 9

Ocean
coast, beach
surfing, snorkeling, swimming
happy, excited, intrigued, content
Sandy

                                  Ryan Lewis

Football
watching, running
sitting, jumping, tackling
drinking, falling
That hurt!

Braden P. Moore
Age: 8

Wind
blowing, invisible
moves, whistles, makes waves
cold, scared, mad, happy
Air

Michael Glockner
Age: 8

Soccer
pushing, shoving
kicking, sliding, running
coaching, playing
I'm hurt! Sit down!

Shelby Kelley
Age: 8

Ricky Martin
cool, neat
singing, dancing, listening
He sings all night long.

Chelsea Adams
Age: 8

Courtney
nice, fun
helping, caring, loving
I love to be kind.

Courtney Davis
Age: 8

WINTER

I am so glad to hear!
   That winter is near!
I like to drink hot cocoa.
   Sometimes in the snow!
Winter is fun for every girl and boy!
   Winter is a joy!

Paige Chandler

WINTER

In winter weather
snowballs fly so high outside
and people ice-skate.

> Brianna Lung
> Age: 12

My dad likes to play
In LA
My dad doesn't drink,
But he likes to blink.
My dad is bored
By watching his Ford.

> Taylor William Garrett
> Age: 8

C aring makes you have friends.
A ll of my friends are nice.
R emember them.
I mportant one.
N otice them.
G ather and make friends.

        Megan Troxell

E ven try your best.
F airness is effort.
F ollow the rules.
O pen books and try your best.
R eally try to put a lot of effort.
T here is effort in your work.

        Cody Allen Rose

BASKETBALL

Basketball, basketball is so fun.
I like my teammates and coach.
We all have goals to achieve and responsibilities.
We have to practice before games.

At games we work hard.
We win and we lose.
At the championship game,
We achieved our goals.
And then we celebrate!

Paige Pfeffer
Age: 11

SPRING

Spring is warm
and leaves turn colors.
It smells fresh and clean.
It tastes like apple pie.
It sounds like birds
are singing a tune.
It reminds me
of my sister's birthday.
Spring makes me feel
happy and safe.

Alicia Rose Hall
Age: 8

SUMMER STORM

The wind whistles through the trees
like harmonious flutes singing their hearts out.

Dark rain-packed clouds hover over the arid plains
as dragonflies to warm waters.

Roaring thunder makes known what's to come
like wild elephant herds stampeding senselessly.

The CRASH of vicious lightning illuminating all
in the path of the grayish ghost
as fires to endangered tropical rain forests.

Animals of nature scatter for shelter frenziedly
like the diffusion of passionate perfume.

Magically, the turbulence is silently stilled
as flowers knowing when it's time to wane away
for winter.

Beautifully, the rising of the sun brings life
to a new day like the dawning of springtime.

Zachary M. Cochran
Age: 16

Happiness is yellow.
It sounds like kids laughing.
It smells like cinnamon.
It tastes like chocolate.
It looks like playing
Happiness feels like fun.

Megan Elizabeth Berberich
Age: 8

C hristmastimes are fun.
H ides all the time.
R emember he is real.
I love him.
S ome people say Santa is real.
T oday is not CHRISTMAS.
M any people never see him.
A present here and there.
S ome are big and small.

Joshua R. Faul

FALL

Fall is beautiful, fall is bold,
  Fall is yellow, red, and gold.
Hayrides on a farmer's wagon,
  Children dressed as spooks and dragons.
Thanksgiving meals we all enjoy,
  Food for every girl and boy.
Fall is beautiful, fall is bold,
  So much beauty to behold.

Terry Schram
Age: 12

CHRISTMAS

It's Christmas! Oh my!
It's Christmas Eve!
My sister and I can't sleep,
Santa is coming!

It's Christmas Day!
We go downstairs,
There are presents underneath the tree
It's Christmas! Oh, my!

Tabitha Rickey
Age: 12

JOY

Joy to me is happiness,
Also love and hope,
Would you be my joy?
Joy to me is you.

Ashley McFarland
Age: 12

HALLOWEEN

Halloween, Halloween
The scariest season of all.
It only comes once a year,
always in the fall.
Kids dress up for trick-or-treat
and go from door-to-door.
They ask for something good to eat
and hurry on for more.
If you run out,
you better find something quick!
Because if you don't,
you might get a nasty trick.
Halloween, Halloween
the funnest season of all
so go out and get dressed up
and really have a ball!

Jessica Ann Salisbury

MOTHERS

Mothers are wonderful things.
They are God's way of saying "I love you,"
And they push you to succeed.

They guide you to the right place,
Always thinking of your good,
Never letting you go wrong.

They love you with all your hearts,
Making you even more special every day,
They encourage you to do right.

They keep you from failing,
Always there for you,
Just knowing what to do.

Mothers are bright and beautiful,
Loving, tender, sweet, and caring,
Mothers are wonderful things.

                                        Alanna Zimmerman

SLEEPOVERS

I love sleepovers,
We stay up late
And watch movies.
Curl our hair
Or play truth or dare.
I wish there was a rule
All sleepovers, no school!
But until then,
Every weekend is fine with me
Too bad it will never be the rule
Of all sleepovers, no school.

Brittany Merice
Age: 12

CLOUDS

Clouds are black, gray, and white
Sometimes they aren't in sight
Some clouds are tall
Others are very small
Clouds are crystals in the sky
Some fly so very high

Kelsey Isfort
Age: 8

SNOW SNOW

Snow snow I love it when you come
and cancel school.
Snow snow when you hit my face
you are very cool.
Snow snow you rule!!

Snow snow I hate it when you melt
and that's what I hate
because trust me,
Snow snow it's a very long wait.

Justin Telfor
Age: 12

SOCCER

Soccer is cool!
Soccer is neat!
Soccer is when you run.
Soccer is when you can get beat.
I love soccer!
Because my kicks are sweet!
Plus this poem is complete.

Allyson Martin
Age: 12

WHERE I'M FROM

I am from glasses,
   from Brunco wood stoves and Stihl chain saws.
I am from the wooden floor boards of my bedroom,
   (Shiny and dark, smooth to the touch.)
I am from the pine trees,
   the tulips:
     towering and wide.
I'm from warm winter nights and dark straight hair,
   from Gary
     and Tammy.
I'm from the avid readers, and the "Faster fasters!"
   from a wounded soldier,
     and motorcycle trips.
I'm from a minister's son,
   from a dinner prayer
I'm from Georgetown and Germany
   from pancakes and chocolate cheesecakes,
   from the sailboats on Lake Cowan
   built by my family,
     the cottage tended by my grandmother,
       the shelf of photo albums,
       the black leather chair,
         the whole glorious family
         before me and around me.

Alex Silvis
Age: 13

THE FIELD

In the winter,
the field is like a hibernating white polar bear.
It just sits there, flat and still,
a lonely wind blowing over it.

In the spring,
the field is thawing like a pack of hamburger.
It is filled with people hoeing and plowing
like a small army making trenches,
a canvas waiting for the painter to begin.

In the summer,
the field is like an old piece of toast
with mold on top.
It is filled with green growing crops
growing as fast as weeds do.

In the fall,
the field is like a golden bar
spanning over the flat land.
It is filled with the golden fruits
of a finished harvest season.

And now, we're back to winter, flat, white, still.

Cody Clifton
Age: 12

I have a funny pumpkin
Who sings "Where is Thumbkin?"
He has a funny face,
But he doesn't have a shoelace.
His hair is made of leaves,
And his mouth is made of peas.

Rebecca Hall
Age: 9

SUMMER

Out of school
Crystal blue pools
Trying for swimming champ
While I'm stuck at camp

Tiffany A. McIntosh

ASTRONAUT

Astronaut, astronaut
I want to be an astronaut.
I want to fly in outer space.
I want to land on the moon.
I hope I can do it soon.

Brian James Cochran
Age: 11

THE CAR

Once there was a boy named Steven
Who told everyone he was leavin'
He ran so far,
But got hit by a car
And now he's in bed bleedin'.

Stephen Girshovich

DIGIMON

Digimon are digital monsters.
They live in Digiworld.
Digimon are to protect people
from evil Digimon
not just any people but seven kids
that are knocked into Digiworld.
Then the kids get digivices
to make their Digimon digivolve.
When they digivolve nothing can stop them.
Then the kids have to find crest
so their Digimon can digivolve
to the ultimate level
and beat evil Digimon.

Robert M. Pearl
Age: 10

My pumpkin has a hat,
And for lunch he eats a gnat.
He lives in LA,
And he does not like ballet.
He has a frog,
But he does not like fog.

Emily Lodwick
Age: 8

HELP

If my people need help
I'll give them help.
I fly across the river.
I'll take the bus
I'll fly a jet.
I stand up high.
If my people go down
I'll pull them up.
My people need help.
My people need help
And I'll be there 'cause I am the hero!

Tonika Jonnell Pope
Age: 12

My pumpkin is very nice,
But all of her friends are field mice.
She likes the rain,
She also likes her train.
She is very rotten,
Her hair is as soft as cotton.
Her favorite food is spaghetti,
Her best friend is Eddie.

Katelyn Taylor
Age: 8

JONDS

Hands thin and lanky
Like Scooby-Doo's Shaggy
But still strong and veiny
Like the guy on Muscle Mania

Slight knuckle hair
Like the brownest brown bear
Knuckles full of love and care
But can still rip and tear

Black magic fills his hand
Such effective grains of sand
This takes him to his land
Were he can fly and

Fall

In this concrete jungle
Where his hands must always struggle
For he has no body double
And his problems only he can juggle

"Where you want to go next?
Over to the bank complex?"
"Sure my life's complex
Don't worry you'll get there yet."

Nick Warndorff

ANNE FRANK

Anne Frank was a Jew
Born in Germany during World War II
The Germans wanted to kill the Jews
Thanks to Adolph Hitler, a killer,
He thought of the news
Anne's family was quite scared
And the rules they had to follow were not fair
Anne was forced into hiding for two years
Which was illegal to talk, be seen, or hear
In 1945, Anne and her family got caught
They were sent to a slave camp,
And it wasn't very hot
Now World War II was almost over
Germany was in a battle with Russia,
The country next door
Anne Frank died at age fifteen
Just a few weeks before the Russians came
To set the Jews free
Anne's father had survived the war
When he heard the sad news about his wife,
Daughter, and Anne,
He read Anne's diary over
A year later, it was published
So now, when I think of Anne, I say,
"No more race hatred rubbish"

Suzanne Buzek
Age: 10

ABRAHAM LINCOLN

Abraham Lincoln was a hardworking guy.
He even worked hard when he was knee-high.
He had to work hard for the little he had,
All that he had went straight to his dad.
He was first elected president in 1861.
You can't imagine all of the jobs that he had done.
A boatman, a postman just to name a few.
There wasn't anything good
That "Honest Abe" wouldn't do.
Abraham Lincoln when speaking always impressed,
Especially when he gave the Gettysburg Address.
He led the Union Army into the Civil War,
He prayed and prayed that it wouldn't go far.
They fought the war until 1865.
He said the Gettysburg Address
For those who had died.
He went to the theater one evening to see a play,
Little did he know that it would be his last day.
Although too early he went to his grave,
He will always be known
As the man who freed the slaves.
Today Americans still honor his name,
For the great American president that he became.

Kevin Waklatsi
Age: 10

MIA HAMM

My name is Mariel Hamm
But I prefer Mia,
I like it much better
Than Caitlin or Leah!

My mom's heart was set
On tap and ballet,
But I had something different
In mind I'll say!

As a child of an Air Force colonel
I was a military brat.
My family moved often
From this place to that!

Moving all over
Is difficult too
Always making new friends
Is what I had to do!

So playing sports
Would help me make friends,
And I would keep in touch
With the latest sports trends.

Playing basketball and soccer
Would bring me joy.
Did I play with the girls?
No, I preferred the boys!

My brother Garrett
Would always pick me.

He said for a girl
I played with intensity!

Garrett was very special,
An inspiration, you see.
When he died
I lost a big part of me!

I know that he would
Really like,
That I put his initials
On my soccer cleat by Nike!

As I got older
Soccer became my game.
I played so hard
People thought I was insane!

I played for the Sidewinders
When I was a kid.
I played for the Tar Heels
When I got big!

Now I play
With the very best!
I play with Chastain, Scurry
And all the rest!

I've won NCAA Championships
I've won the World Cup!
I have a gold medal
I've been nowhere but up!

Soccer is fun,
And it has taught me,
To play as a team
And with dignity!

Win or lose,
Always give your best,
Not just in soccer
But in all life's tests!!

Caitlin Thompson
Age: 10

BETSY ROSS

Betsy Ross lived an interesting life
She was a sister, a mother, a sewer and a wife
Betsy had seventeen sisters and brothers
She worked in an upholstery shop with many others
Husbands she had three
She had been a widow twice you see
Children she had seven
While she was alive two were in Heaven
As the war went by
Prices got very high
But Betsy sewed more
Making uniforms for soldiers in the war
The thing about Betsy we will always remember
She sewed the stars and stripes that will fly forever

Kelsey Vehr
Age: 10

INNER WAR

One man left,
In a war against many.
One man left,
In a war against one.
A battle for blood.
A battle for peace.
One man left,
In a war waged within.
One man left,
To win all the answers
A war against himself.

Jacob Zimmer
Age: 15

TIME

Time is a powerful thing,
controlling the past, present, and future,
and the now, the then and the later.
All day, all the time,
you can find time,
because it's always here,
it's always there,
and it will never be the same.

Adam J. Wanninger
Age: 11

LAURA INGALLS

Laura Ingalls is my name
   And this is how I got my fame
I lived in a cabin in the Big Woods
   And we didn't have too many goods
My ma and pa traveled quite far
   And they didn't even own a car
Ma cooked and sewed and kept a clean house
   Pa hunted and farmed and was a good spouse
My sisters were Mary, Carrie, and Grace
   And we made quilts that were covered with lace
We lived in a house that was made of sod
   The prairie had grass and the creek had cod
Pa told stories and I liked to write
   And that's what we did in the dark of the night
Often in the winter, the blizzards were cold
   It helped that Pa grew wheat to be sold
Mary caught a fever, which was such a fright
   And as a result she lost her eyesight
I was a good student, who decided to teach
   I missed my family, when they weren't within reach
My hero was Manly, who helped save the town
   He asked me to marry him and I wore a gown
The times were improving and I had a child
   Her name was Rose, for flowers that are wild
I became an author, for children to see
   How the history of America, came to be

Allison Luginbill
Age: 10

WINTER

Freezing cold winter
snow, ice, icicles, harvesting
and everything is dead

Richard Herbolt
Age: 12

He has eyes so beady,
Beady as can be.
He is fat,
But is so phat.
Nice and swell,
But someone might throw him in a well.

Dylan Ketchum
Age: 9

WINTER

Winter is very cold and blue,
Snowball fights are not new,
In winter you can eat long pieces of ice,
You also can put the ice in your hot cocoa
And watch for mice,
But I will not scream at a small mouse.

Sometimes a snowdrift will come up to your door,
And you will see a big pile of snow on your floor.
You can throw up some snowflakes,
And they will make a snow fort,
You will have a reward for your effort --
The mouse will be snug in its warm little house.

Martha K. Esslinger
Age: 13

STOP, STOP, STOP

Stop, stop, stop hurry up
get to school chop, chop, chop.
Stop, stop, stop hurry up
get to work chop, chop, chop.
Stop, stop, stop hurry up
get to the store chop, chop, chop.
Stop, stop, stop hurry up
get to bed rest, rest, rest.

Kendra Bush
Age: 11

Chris
Daring,
Champion,
Nice,
Wishes to fly like an eagle,
Dreams of having an Irish wolfhound.
Wants to work for a good company.
Who wonders what life is going to be like.
Who fears getting shot.
Who is afraid of tigers.
Who likes big dogs.
Who believes in UFO's and aliens.
Who loves pineapple and ham pizza.
Who loves to play football.
Who loves to look at spiders.
Who loves to study snakes.
Who plans to get a dirt bike.
Who plans to get a nice car.
Who plans to be successful.
Whose final destination is Heaven.

Christopher Hale
Age: 12

DESIRE AND DETERMINATION
BRING ANY GOAL WITHIN REACH

Paris
Sweet,
Touching,
Athletic,
Wishes to live in a huge house,
Dreams of living in Hawaii,
Who wonders what other planets really look like.
Who fears heights.
Who is afraid of fire.
Who believes in God.
Who loves cake and ice cream.
Who loves to swim.
Who loves teachers, especially Mrs. Georgostathis.
Who loves spaghetti and meatballs.
Who plans to be a swimmer.
Who plans to have children.
Who plans to live a long time.
Whose final destination is Heaven.

Paris Nelson Witt
Age: 10

MOM AND I

I am like a strawberry, wild and fresh.
  My mom is like a car, that needs gas.
I am like a gold mine, I have lots to offer,
  My mom is like a mouse, always sneaky,
Together we are wise, loving and caring.

Destiny Marie Ooten
Age: 10

SUSAN B. ANTHONY

Her name was Susan B. Anthony
She worked hard all her life
To make women free

Susan B. was born in 1820
For the women of our country
She did plenty

In Susan B. Anthony's day
"Women are not equal"
The men would say

It was Susan B. Anthony that wrote
The words giving all women
The right to vote

Laura Elizabeth Apel
Age: 10

ALISTAIR'S HANDS

With a little bit of red dust stuck beneath them,
my brother's nails are round,
and deeply ridged like a rippling tide.
Careful, steady, and wise
they grip onto unsafe rocks and dead roots.

His hands look ancient,
like an old man with some unforetold wisdom
even he is unaware of.
And young, like a fresh newborn baby
who clenches his fist tight against the world,
waiting for his touch.

Little muscles flex as his hands,
dry like a swatch of old leather,
and wrinkled with curiosity,
work hard to support his body,
pulling it up the side of a deathly dry wall
of sand and limestone.

I am focused on the hands working,
my little brother coming up from beneath me.
"Alistair, where are we going?"
out of breath I heave the words.
Looking at me,
with beady eyes and a shock of blond
over his stern expression: "I don't know..."

His hands quiver,
for one moment his fingers debate,
then secure themselves onto a twisting vine.
He continues on ahead.

Up out of the shadow
created by the giant rock, he climbs.

His right hand is illuminated, one filthy hand.
Scratched with the rips of struggle
and hanging loose with the satisfaction
of a job well done.
Then his left hand meets the sunlight too.
One last effort and my brother peers out
onto the tumbling canyons splotched with juniper.

He looks at his palms
calloused with the accomplishments
of climbing a mountain.
Lips curl a little
and I wonder if he's noticed that they match
the color of the red dirt.

Jasmine Probst
Age: 16

FIRE FIRE

Fire fire that's the name
come on and dance you got the flame.
Fire fire is not very fun.
Fireman deputy either one.
Fire fire is in the house
hurry man come get it out.
Fire fire is everywhere
it gave me a great big scare
yellow, orange, and red too
are the colors of my favorite shoes.

C. Patrick Brown
Age: 10

WAR'S CRY

Wars are fought with two sides at battle.
Desperate cries reach desperate measures.
Passion with love and passion with hate,
Can bring about a person's fate.
Embracing the new, breaking the old,
Crumbling the tension, ripping death's hold.
Taking away what used to be,
And now nothing more than a sprouting seed.

Amy Fitzgerald
Age: 13

BOOKS

Books are our imagination
You learn, have fun, and get excited
If you like, you can go anywhere

Jonathan Robinson
Age: 10

TEARS OF BEAUTY

Lipstick red and pink
I dropped mascara in the sink
It splattered in my eye
Which makes me want to cry
But I don't turn to mush
Because I still have to put on blush

When I step into my room
Outside flowers begin to bloom
I look at my sweaters cool and wool
I'm not happy 'til my drawer is full

I'm as beautiful as a butterfly
When I walk down the street people say "Oh my!"
Now that's the end of my rhyme
Uh, oh got to go it's my bedtime

Lyntra M. Eves
Age: 10

RUNNING DOWN HER STREETS

she runs instinctively from her life
she sees her reality,
one which is so much bigger than herself
she sees scars on her pinkish flesh;
her painful reflection in the mirror
and the more she sees the smaller she seems,
among the bigger reality,
and she herself gets lost inside.

lost among feelings she can't describe;
all of her stabbing questions
their answers lost among the streets
so she sprints away from herself;
down the block and then some
chasing the answers,
fearing that if she doesn't run fast enough
the answers will elude her for many more years.

she passes familiar smells and faces
faces similar to the one she once had,
before hers turned a stone cold gray.
she passes lost ways and mistakes
that she will never regret making
she only regrets letting failure rule her life

she needs answers to the whys and hows
and whos and whens of her life;
of her frustration; confusion;
she tries to outrun the judgments
spawned by her mistakes
but they outrun her in the end.

she trips, falling to her hands and knees,
once again, hitting the cold hard pavement.
another scrape and bruise and tear;
another shot to her failing ego
this, the last time she will accept the fall
for the next time she will balance herself on two feet
walking away with a little more confidence
than she came with.

Tess Warner
Age: 16

DISNEY'S DREAM

Walt Disney was a man
  who had a great big plan
He was part of a team
  that would fulfill his dream
A dream to entertain
  with movies, fun and trains
Kids and adults the same
  would all enjoy his game
With great imagination he built his park
  so we could have fun until way past dark
Even though he's not here
  his ideas still give us cheer

Samantha Davenport
Age: 10

BEAUTIFUL BUTTERFLY

I would love to know
how it feels
to be a butterfly.

To feel the wind,
rushing under my wings
and embracing me
with gentle hands
like those of a mother
holding her newborn child
for the first time.

All the other animals
would envy
my wonderful wings,
but I would not boast.
I would just smile and fly by.

I would hold my head up high
and smile,
knowing that I could do
whatever I wanted.

To be a butterfly.

Katie Dale
Age: 15

NOPE

I put a piece of cantaloupe,
Underneath the microscope.
I saw a million strange things sleepin',
I saw a zillion weird things creepin'.
I saw some green things twist and bend,
I won't eat cantaloupe again.

Briddia Murray
Age: 7

SILVERY MOON

The moon washes the earth
With a pale, silvery light,
And lights the world aglow.
That silvery crescent in the sky
Has mystical secrets untold.
The man within it looks down upon us
And keeps a watchful eye;
His presence remains throughout the night,
'Til he flees in secret from the sky.

Chrissy Callan

I

APPLES

Apples red and apples green
Falling to the ground,
Julia eats them, ripe and clean
Her hunger then cannot be found

Apples delight,
Apples Braeburn,
Apples you eat at night
Bob for apples, wait your turn.

Apples red and apples green
Falling to the ground,
Julia craves them sight unseen
Yum yum yum yum is the sound.

Julia Donnelly
Age: 9

I look to my left
I look to my right
I see cars a-coming
I look to my left
I look to my right
I guess it is safe to cross the street

Stefen Marquis Smith

SORROW VERSUS JOY

Sorrow is black
It smells like rubber burning
It tastes like deep-fried mushrooms
It sounds like silence
It feels like open-heart surgery
It looks like a bottomless pit
Sorrow is a lost soul

Joy is lavender
It smells like a florist's shop
It tastes like cotton candy
It sounds like a soft, sweet, harmony
It feels like Heaven
It looks like fluffy puppies
Joy is an endless emotion.

Jennifer Nicole Van Fleet
Age: 13

TV

The television set is in the living room
My dad thinks it will bring us to our doom
I watch TV day in and day out
When my dad gets home he always shouts
He gets in the TV's way and says
"Back in my day..."

Jim O'Brien
Age: 13

FRIENDS

Friends are people whom you can meet,
Even on a paper sheet.

Friends are people who really know,
Especially when you are low.

They understand every day,
In each and every special way.

Friends help you decide what's right and wrong,
If you choose wrong, they don't play along.

Friends don't get mad,
Unless you do something really bad.

Friends can sense when you want to be alone,
Like they had already known.

I have some friends who aren't the best,
But they're still like all the rest.

I know I've had a friend
That I thought was really cool,
But at the end, they were nothing but a fool.

A friend is someone who thinks you're cool,
And takes no one for a fool.

Friends have their ups and downs,
But never, ever turn around.

A friendship should never break,
Even though it just might shake.

Friends are people who never hide,
They always stick by your side.

If someone does something wrong,
Friends should make it clear just like a gong.

Some are the best, some are the worst,
Some even act like they have been cursed.

Friends are different and that is no lie,
But most of those differences
Should squeak right by.

I'm not the best and neither are you,
But you should try to be, no matter what you do.

Somewhere out there I have a perfect friend,
I must go through a lot of bends
To find that perfect friend!

Jennifer Hester
Age: 11

THE OREGON TRAIL

Wagons winding through the hills
And across the open prairie
Campfires light the ground
Children laughing and playing
In the meadow grasses

Rachel Martin
Age: 8

RUDE AWAKENING

I feel tired and just a little sleepy
my eyes are wilting and just a little weepy
I crawl into bed and do not object
in my head dreams a project
I could be a princess
I could be a queen
I love to dream where all can be seen
In the distance I hear a faint sound
in my head things go 'round and 'round
I see a light and smell pancakes and bacon
I feel all my dreams have been taken
But I am not tired or just a little sleepy
my eyes aren't wilting or at all weepy
It will happen again today
I will be tired at the end of the day.

Abby Bowden
Age: 12

I DREAM

I dream --
I dream of life,
Of things I do;
I dream of school
And hostile takeovers;
I dream of leading
Or falling down;
I dream I'm a hero
Or swept away;
I dream I can fly
And run back home;
I dream in color,
I dream in emotion;
I run, run, run
With my fear, anger, sadness, glee;
Perfectly normal
But foreign in consciousness.
The dreams rise up,
Distort the topics of life,
Breathe depth to unconsciousness
And fold.
The dreams die;
I am lost.

Carl Sack
Age: 17

HALLOWEEN

H urry!
A t last it's Halloween
L et's give it a shout,
L et's give it a scream!
O pen the coffins,
W inds seem to moan,
E verywhere there are spirits, don't come alone,
E veryone eats the candy on the scene,
N ow, let's hit the streets with our tricks
   and our treats for it is ....
   Halloween!

Rosa M. Lyons
Age: 11

SEASONS

Winter, a snowy day,
Spring, a time to sing,
Summer, a time to get better
Fall, I love best of all!

There are so many seasons,
I can't keep track,
I love all of them,
I hope they all come back!

Kathleen Carney
Age: 10

HARD TIMES

My father unwilling to speak,
To tell his story,
Like the rock,
Unable to tell the story of its life.

I wonder, if their stories were told,
Would anyone care to listen
Or would they be forced to carry on
Frightened by the very things
that created them.

It is so strong and real,
Yet so comforting,
It is nothing like our world,
So full of confusion.

So foreign to what we know,
As if they were from another time,
Striving for comfort,
In a world manufactured by hate.

Stuart Tennison
Age: 16

You call over to me,
Your voice was familiar.
I hear you puffing, breathing
On a Camel,
Filled with hope, you talk;
Not like a brother;
Not like a friend,
But more.
Sacred,
Limited.
I ask if you want Mom,
But you say no
And I smile.
You have traveled
And seen the way
The world works.
Hopped trains,
You once depended on some artificial powder.
But, now you call.
You dial my phone number,
And ask for me.

Chelsea Buncher
Age: 17

NOAH AND THE ARK

God told Noah that a rain is coming
So pack your bags and get a-going
So Noah made an ark that was made of bark
They laughed at him as he built his big ship
They said, "Man, he must be taking a long trip"
It rained for forty days and nights
And the people that were left behind
Were full of fright
After the rain God sent a rainbow as a sign
That he would never do it again

Jordan Bonne
Age: 11

EXPERIMENT

Test tubes, test tubes everywhere!!!
I hope I don't get that stuff in my hair.
What are we experimenting with this time?
I hope it doesn't cost me a dime.

The experiment was a test.
I really tried my best.
I don't know what my grade will be,
I hope it is not a "C"!

Robby Talbott
Age: 10

I

I went to Florida!
I took a plane.

To Epcot I went;
To downtown Disney I went;
To Disney World,
To Animal Kingdom,

I saw
Mickey
And
Minnie
And
Goofy
And
Donald
And
Pluto!

I had a great lunch
With the Disney bunch,
And it was
SO MUCH FUN!
Florida.

Julien Hunter
Age: 9

My cat
is almost three years old,
Oddly enough,
he's very bold.
Black with a blank
spot on his chest,
my cat seems better
than all the rest.
He stays in our house
and tackles string,
Sometimes runs into the
basement where
he'll often scream.
Once ran 'cross the room
and got my dad with twelve claws,
On toast and pancakes
he sometimes gnaws.
My cat's birthday
is on Halloween,
'Though I got him on January seventeen.
If you want a cat who's very strange,
Don't come to us:
We won't exchange!

Kevin Colmar
Age: 10

Dusty beams of piercing sunshine
breaking through the spirals of your hair
not weaving
never breaking a constant endless mission
from here to the never-coming night
stars lighting the sun's mirror of the mystical moon

Forgiving and gentle you brush away
the warm gaze and move on
moving towards the nonexistent
searching for the dry shoulder
that you will never find

Roaring seas flashing electrically, certain
across your stormy eyes lighting rooms
and ways,
paths of the long forgotten friend we mourned
for minutes lost
traversing pebbly itchy yesterdays
forging smiles and firm struts
crossing rivers with air-filled lungs
spitting out bitter memories on the other side
like cutting your baby finger on clean endless
sheets of paper
the blood of the trees: wide as your empty embrace

Petals falling from the green silky leaves
on snowy frosty dawns
the stars dreaming and confused
letting the pink fall streaming down
pouring from the holes in the empty gray skies
down to the sharp merciless

tangles of fairy studded grass

Like bubbles floating over your dirty red car
as you zip by mistaking hungry souls for cacti
that can do on their own
lonely and wandering
burning and stinging their hard feet

And the sunshine dusty and imperfect
searches on for your red lips to curl

Jenna C. Laumer

SCHOOL TODAY

Every day I go to school
Doing my work with all my tools.
Playing with friends
And talking with them.
Today, school is almost over.

I'm ready to run!
And I hope I get home
Before Pokémon
Goes off.

I watch TV
And my homework, I do.

Donte L. Mooney
Age: 9

THE SPOILS OF WAR

Bullets are flying,
And men are dying.
Oh, when will this war end?

Children are crying,
Wives' skillets are frying --
They are crying and cooking
For the men who will never come home.

This endless war has caused the men to die.
This endless war has caused the children to cry.
this endless war has caused wives to wonder why.

Because of this war, the men won't come home.
Because of this war,
The women and children will be left alone.
Oh, when will this war end?

Paige Bradds
Age: 13

SUMMER WIND

Summer wind blowing me
not knowing where or when or why then you reply,
"Here and there now and then
and because it wants to fly!"

Katie Sturgill
Age: 10

This is my classroom
I like my classroom
we write, we learn
we learn how to spell
we write on our board
to do our math
we write on the board
to do our problems
we go to lunch
to eat our food
we eat, we talk,
we come back up
do more work
at 2:00 pm
we all go home
until then
see you later.

Tihiau Carter
Age: 11

MY COUNTRY

The love of my country,
How dear I feel.
I want to hug it and hold it near.
After the war what a gruesome sight;
Seeing the bodies hopelessly in the night.
The blood spouting from the bodies there;
I can tell my country loves thee dear.
I, a drummer boy and nothing else.
I'm nine years old and four feet tall.
No one this young should have to see this all.

Sarah Wortman
Age: 12

Nick
Cool,
Fast,
Loyal,
Wishes to be famous.
Dreams of being a secret agent.
Wants to be a soldier.
Who wonders if aliens exist.
Who fears death.
Who is afraid of the world coming to the end.
Who likes to play soccer.
Who believes in peace.
Who loves bike riding.
Who loves steak and chicken.
Who loves to wrestle.
Who plans to be a soldier.
Who plans to go to Florida.
Who plans to live a healthy life.
Whose final destination is to make peace.

Nicholas Ho
Age: 10

HIS WORDS

His words flew like wood chips,
They fell down,
Filling the room
With sharp words
Falling on me,
Advise, wisdom, direction.

He wanted me to sweep them up
And shove them inside,
Neatly in a pile,
So that I may pull from them
Whatever answers I might need.

He is strong
Like a rock,
Made of thick, condensed pride,
Packed so tight,
No more room in there,
I admire that,
But struggle to understand.

Always strong,
And always willing,
To add his two cents,
His advice often jangles in my head,
That unmistakable sound of his words,
Cover up all the other sounds,
The loud clank,
A constant reminder
Of my father.

He is heavy like a rock,
Heavy with the weight of his own wisdom,
Weighing me down,
Where did all this come from?
I ask myself,
As his words fly like wood chips towards me.

                              Leah K. Busch
                              Age: 16

                Happy is yellow.
                It smells like roses.
                It tastes like candy.
          It sounds like a very pretty song.
                It feels like a cloud.
              It looks like a big smile.
          Happy is a birthday present.

                              Ashley Egbert
                              Age: 11

QUEEN ELIZABETH II

There's a country, green and fair
Called England, and a queen lives there
She was young and pretty too,
When crowned in 1952.

In forty-seven years her reign
Has brought fortune, love and fame,
As she has always been content
To leave government to parliament.

When "Lilibet," the little girl
Was dancing in the social whirl,
None in England dreamed or reckoned
That she'd be Queen Elizabeth the Second.

Elizabeth Coorey
Age: 10

I saw a raindrop.
It dropped on the ground
and made a plop sound.

Jessica Liming
Age: 8

MY HORSE

The mane of my horse is white as snow in winter.
His legs have gray spots.
They are strong to carry me
To the top of mountains.

Courtnie Meehan
Age: 10

THUNDERSTORMS

Boom boom as the thunder roars on
Flash flash as the lightning flashes
on and off like a flashlight
Drop drop as the rain falls on the rusty old barn
Bam bam as the hail stones fall
on the hard cold gray cement
Boom boom -- flash flash -- drop drop --
bam bam as the thunderstorm rages
through the wet cold night.

B. J. Geier
Age: 10

FAMILY SECRETS

Some families have a secret
That they don't want people to know.
It's something that's probably personal,
That you would never tell a soul.
Some close friends might know about it
And some probably may not.
You usually only tell people
That you've known a long time.
When you have a family secret,
And it bothers you a lot,
If you're a Christian,
You probably pray about it to God.

Kellie P. Robinson
Age: 12

I AM A SPECIAL PERSON

I am a special person
You're a special person
You may be the chosen one
You may be the only one
You can be the perfect one
You can be the perfect one
You can be the smartest one
But in your eyes you're the chosen

Courtney Harris
Age: 9

FEELINGS

Sadness is blue.
It sounds like a dog whining.
It smells like an ocean.
It tastes like saltwater.
It looks like a puddle of water.
It feels like no one is on your side.

Mad is dark red.
It sounds like firecrackers.
It smells like a bonfire.
It tastes like a hot pepper.
It looks like you are red.
It feels like hot water on your skin.

Chelsea Marie Kessler
Age: 9

IF I WERE A PUMPKIN

If I were a green pumpkin.
I'd make a funny face and scare people.
I'd turn green and sleep in the garage.
I would run away from the house,
so the kids wouldn't carve me.
That was close.
I will open my top and take their candy
it makes me feel good.

Sam Galeano
Age: 7

A SUCCESSFUL BASKETBALL TEAM

Two coaches
Two teaspoons of hardworking
Three teaspoons of teamwork
Six flexible children
Six jerseys
One basketball court
Eight basketballs

Mix flexible children, nice jerseys,
and two coaches together in one pan.
Pour into another pan and mix basketballs together.
In another pan mix one teaspoon of hardwork
and one teaspoon of teamwork together
and pour into other bowl.
Put on stove and heat for one hour.

Rikhev Kashyap
Age: 9

AUTUMN HIKE

October is a flowing sea
of gentle crinkling waves of leaves
light hazy clouds floating
across the drab yet flushed sky at daybreak
the crystalline frost at my feet
the chill of autumn descends my spine
the cool breeze brushes the tips of my hair
I take shelter in my cottage after a morning hike
a mouthful of steaming cider warms my throat
a crackling shimmering fire awaits me

Dane Holte
Age: 13

IF I WERE A MAGIC SPELL

If I were a magic potion spell...
I'd swirl around and make a colorful brightness.
When the kids come by I'd make them disappear.
I'd put a magic spell on them so they would obey.
Then I would make them dance.
Everybody would be laughing.
I would suck them into my body.
Poof!!! Poof!!!

Kevin Muenks
Age: 7

TORNADO

Boom boom, bang bang,
Crack crash whack wham
Hear the thunder roaring?
A severe thunderstorm,
Listen to the loud roaring.
A blaring siren.
Grab a blanket and a flashlight
Scurry to the basement
A roaring freight train noise,
Sounding like a train traveling
Three hundred miles per hour
Hear the splitting sound of trees cracking
Hitting the roof and the walls

It is finally over
I am ever relieved
Take a look outside and wonder what I'll see
The neighbor's roof caved in.
Our car smashed
Trees knocked down on the roof
Denting the roof
Pieces of twisted metal
Wrapped around the trees left standing
Clothing and sheets strangled by the trees

Cleanup has finally begun
Things scattered all around
Find baseball cards

Find toys and books
Find irreplaceable pictures

Devastating tornado has wreaked chaos on life
I want to get through survival to normalcy

Andrew Wittkugel

SECOND-GRADE WORMS

They wiggle and squiggle,
all in a patch,
from the north to the south,
then all the way back.
They jiggle and twiggle
and stir about,
I teach second-grade worms,
there is no doubt!

Natalie J. Watson
Age: 7

B ikes are cool
I like bikes
K eep bikes in the garage
E very bike has brakes
S ome bikes have shocks

Donald Moore

BATHTUB

This claw-footed monster
is one of the most feared creatures in the world.
It sucks up water and spits it back out of its mouth.
So be careful, because if you let your guard down
he'll soak you with water and eat you up.
But I usually don't think about this
when I use him every night.

Stephen Vonderwish

SIXTEEN

To be young and sixteen
Is to be reckless;
Learning lessons the hard way
Grieving and regretting.

To be young and sixteen
Is to be stubborn and stupid;
Not listening to the wise advice given
Ignoring your elders.

Causing problems
But yet growing,
Inside and outside
Maturing and preparing to face the world.

Not realizing our mortality
Feeling as though we are nearly invincible,
As did Phaethon before he destroyed the earth
Someday I hope we'll realize.

           Katie Sullivan

POWER

Power is a harsh responsibility,
It is doing and speaking
With knowledge.

Power is bidding without
thought and knowing
that one will be obeyed.

When the power is gone
You are left in peace.
The doves on the wall,
The sun, and the moon
become the world
as you sit and watch.

Power is not sight;
It is more than that.
Everyone has sight,
But few possess power
Like Zeus ruling
the immortal beings.

Power is a harsh gift,
which has left me in peace.

I do not look back and wish otherwise
For now I know that the power I possessed
Was not mine to keep.

Colleen Everett

500 FREESTYLE

The time has come.
Before, I have gone through this.
Many times before.
And I am still nervous.
I take off my towel,
Shivering in my wet suit.
The crowd cheers as I adjust my goggles,
And the man says step up.
I breathe deeply and try to reassure myself.
It's okay, you're fine.
The beep sounds,
I'm off with a leap
Head first into freezing water.
I fall into the pattern;
Up, back; up, back.
The numbers flash by.
Five, nine, thirteen.
Seventeen -- I'm nearly done.
Pulling, I force my arms to go faster.
A girl is only slightly ahead.
Can I beat her?
I scarcely breathe,
Wanting to go faster.
Though I swim through the valley
Of the shadow of death
I fear no evil.
For I can beat her.
The color red flashes before my eyes.
Just one more lap!
I look over and see my competition
Falling closer to me.
With a spurt of speed,

I leave her in my bubbles.
I punch the wall and look up.
Lane 2: 5th place
Lane 1: 6th place
I have won!
I beat the girl!
I crawl out, breathless...
I am ecstatic.
My enemies shall not exult over me.

Melissa Pansing

SUNRISE OF MEMORIES

There is a mist above the horizon,
Light spreads slowly over the lake,
The new sun fills my heart,
As both it and I awake.

I always loved the mountains,
Which is why I am here,
To see all the seasons,
Every single year.

And when I leave these crystal mountains,
And this misty lake,
I know I will sorrow,
For my happiness will quake.

Sarah Loftus
Age: 11

REVIVAL

Golden rays of light illuminate the earth
Bringing warmth and encouraging birth
Melting ice crystals and blankets of snow
Making a path for new life to grow

The trees skinless fingers are no longer bare
The scent of revival drifts through the air
Rivers, once frozen, now trickle and flow
Swirling around bends and turns as they go

The wind, itself, is a mischievous child
With gusts that are strong, playful and wild
The cool breeze whispers and tousles my hair
Racing through life like a swift-footed mare

Green blades of grass have the strength to stand tall
Facing harsh weather and enduring it all
Soft buds are bursting on the branches of trees
Proclaiming survival from the cold winter freeze

Blossoming flowers are pink, violet, maroon
A butterfly emerges from its silky cocoon
It disappears into the clear azure sky
As wispy white clouds roll lazily by

All around me I find that new life is waking
Producing a world that is serene and breathtaking
A choir of bluebirds begin to sing
Announcing the arrival of the season of spring

Linda Elizabeth Kamen
Age: 13

FALLING TO THE GROUND

Falling from the sky
Swaying side to side.
The wind I know will take me
To the place I long to be.

I see what is all around me
Above, below, and beyond.
The sun shining brightly
The children playing cheerfully
The future holds what will come.

The great big master has let me go
Where I fall I will never know.
To the ground, on a street
The mystery is at hand.

I see my destiny to the ground
Where all the kids are playing.
Walking on my friends
I hear their pain and crying.

Falling, floating to the ground
From that great big oak tree
I saw my world around me
Which I am accustomed to love.

The little leaf I am
I have no importance
But I'll do the best I can
To fulfill what God has told me.

Martha Craft
Age: 13

TORNADO APPROACHING

The lights were on,
and then they went out.
the sirens blared,
"watch out, watch out,"

Go down to your cellars,
lie down on your floors,
stay clear of your windows,
and porches, and doors,

And then in a moment,
the winds started swirling,
then came the tornado,
with funnel clouds twirling,

It came with such power,
and brought us such fear,
we huddled together,
to pray and be near,

Then all of a sudden,
the tornado passed,
we climbed from the basement,
to daylight at last,

Some people were injured,
and some lost forever,
we all asked God's love,
to bring us together.

Sarah Trucksis

WINTER

She whispers, gentle, in my ear
As frost rolled off her lips.
And I felt the thrill of winter
As she ran her icey fingertips
Along natures rocky backbone.

The trees turned black.
The sky fell gray,
As her spirit descended
Upon its prey.
I feel the chill of winter.

White, with each breath
She is stealing fragments
Of every warm memory.
Wanting life to stand, stagnent.
A beautiful, cold, picture.

Does she know, I wonder,
With every breath, intake,
I can taste her secrets?
With each perfect snowflake
I melt winter on my tongue.

Andrea Dennis
Age: 17

A GOOD FRIENDSHIP

Ingredients:

One gallon of respect
Two friends
One pint of trust
A touch of love
Half a cup of playing
One pint of cheerfulness
Half a cup of consideration
One dash of communication
One hundred gallons of happiness

Blend two friends.
Add a touch of love and stir with trust.
Bake with consideration and interacting.
Ice with love, happiness, communication,
and playing in the middle.
Set cheerfulness on top.
Serve it with respect for a good friendship.

Chethan Vinay Ramprasad
Age: 9

Marcey
Loving,
Funny,
Friendly.
Wishes to live with 'N Sync,
Dreams of being an artist,
Wants to be with my family.
Who wonders if the world is ever going to end.
Who likes boys that are nice to me.
Who believes in God.
Who loves my family.
Who loves candy.
Who loves school and basketball.
Who plans to be a school teacher.
Who plans to be a mother.
Who plans to have a great life.
Who already has a great life all of the time.

Marcey Spitznagel
Age: 11

Sam Haynes
Happy,
Nice,
Careful.
Wishes to be a football player,
Dreams of being in NASCAR,
Wants to speak out.
Who wonders about school.
Who fears robbers.
Who likes Halloween.
Who likes school.
Who loves math.
Who loves sports.
Who loves food.
Who loves bikes.
Who plans to have fun.
Who plans to ride rides.
Who plans to win.
I love sports.

Samuel A. Haynes
Age: 10

Josh
Careful,
Funny,
Nice.
Wishes to get a python,
Dreams of playing for the Reds,
Wants to try to make people understand
Things of life.
Who wonders about everything.
Who fears going to the doctor.
Who is afraid of the bad people.
Who likes school.
Who believes in Jesus.
Who loves girls.
Who loves baseball.
Who loves dogs and cats.
Who plans to marry Samantha G.
Who plans to play for the Reds.
Who plans to be famous.

                                                Joshua Miranda
                                                       Age: 9

ANDRE AGASSI

Andre Agassi is his name,
tennis is his game.
He started at six,
he learned lots of tricks.
His serve was one hundred miles per hour,
man, that's a lot of power!
At seven he started tournament play,
he had to practice every day.
He was sixteen when he started pro,
when he played he put on a good show.
When he was twenty-six years old,
he went to the Olympics and won the gold.
That same year he came to Cincinnati,
and won the ATP!

Eddie Taylor
Age: 10

IT'S FALL

It's fall
It's fall
I am a bird.
Flying, flapping, falling.
Flying and flapping makes me tired so I go to sleep.
I'm in the air then I will start falling to the ground.
I wish I would not get tired in the air.

Jessica Davis
Age: 7

Brandy
Loving,
Caring,
Thoughtful.
Wishes to have people respect her,
Dreams of having many friends,
Wants to feel more nice.
Who wonders why many people are poor.
Who fears being the youngest.
Who is afraid of murderers.
Who likes pizza with green olives.
Who believes in miracles.
Who loves pizza.
Who loves swimming.
Who loves soccer.
Who loves to make new friends.
Who plans to travel far.
Who plans to keep all friends.
Who plans to be a good friend.
Who plans to save animals.
Wants to be a good friend.

Brandy Kautz
Age: 9

COPING WITH A LOSS

As I watched my aunt lie there
Struggling to live
My heart filled with anger
As tears streamed down my cheeks
Why was God taking her away from me?
I could not understand
I hoped for a miracle
To keep her alive
But as I tightly squeezed her cold hand
I knew those were her final minutes
Her cancer was like Goliath
Only this time, David could not defeat him
I prayed to the angels above
To take care of her in Heaven
Though my aunt is now gone
The memories I have
Of times we shared
Can never be forgotten

Katie Schneider

THE EYE OF GOD

Wind is an invisible sound
Lifting new seeds
Off trees
Calming the destruction
Wrought by evil.

The sun is a solitary
Bright star,
Giving life to reaching plants
Warming the earth with
Its gentle fingers.

Clouds are like pieces of cotton
Pouring forth refreshing
Spring rain
Blotting out the brightness
Of the sky.

Rain is full of
Precious stones
Leaving the world to glisten
Cleansing the dirty cities
Replenishing the dry.

The moon is the eye of God
Soothing the fears of darkness
Smiling down on his creations
Giving hope for a peaceful night.

Holly Lewis

MOST MEMORABLE DAY

I flew through the air
Like Hermes with his winged sandals
When I came down, something was wrong
I hit the ground hard and then heard a snap
I tried to get up but my neck would not move
The ball I once had, began to roll away
I stopped struggling, and lay still
With the smell of grass
All I could do was lie on my side

Focusing on a tall white building
I wanted to cry,
but something told me to hold on... to be strong
A stranger asked me what was wrong
But before I could say, someone screamed
"What's coming out of his arm?"
I became scared,
frantically trying to see what was wrong
But all I could do was lie on my side

The stranger poked at my arm,
which caused excruciating pain
The stranger then began to wrap my arms
and chest tightly together
After finishing, he called someone else over to me
Together, they lifted me up to my knees
From there, I stood up on my own
still not able to see the problem
I walked away thinking I would never return

I was shown slowly to a car
All of the way to the hospital

I felt something moving out of place
I heard the doctors saying,
"You don't see something like that everyday,"
Finally, I looked into a mirror
and saw a bone poking almost through the skin
"All we can do is operate;"
Still thinking I would never return to my passion

I woke up from surgery,
and my arm burned and stung
I wanted it all to end
But it went on so much longer
But through weeks of pain and rehabilitation
I returned to my passion
Because for me soccer is life

Nick Spurlock

Softball
enjoying, playing
hitting, catching, running
throwing, fielding
Winning!

Tiffany Dawn Latham
Age: 9

TREES

Falling yellow leaves
bright green, red, orange, golden brown --
Crunchy, soggy leaves.

Weathenia Morrish

THE BIRTH OF JESUS

A Jewish lady Mary was going to give birth
to her firstborn son.
Her son is greater than anyone.
She went with Joseph to an Inn.
To give birth to her son who will never sin.
There was no room in the Inn
for Joseph and Mary to stay.
So they went to the barn in the back of the Inn
and wrapped him in a cloth and set him to lay.
That night shepherds came and wisemen too.
For that son will always love you,
no matter what you do!
Eight days later they gave him a name,
the name that an angel told Mary, JESUS
I am so glad he came!

Lindsey Ross Parker
Age: 11

M motivated minor
I informational individual
C courteous child
H humorous human
A able athlete
E energetic enigma
L loving lad

>Michael Herrle
>Age: 10

LOST

Lost, surrounded by eternal blackness
Hungry, lacking nourishment and lacking strength
Entrapped by dark figures
Whose limbs scrape the sky
Losing feeling in my legs, there is no way out
Rivers of tears pouring from my face,
Blood running from my legs,
As teethed bushes tear at my flesh
Clouds pour from my mouth,
I no longer feel my hands
My stomach cries out for food
The pain grows too intense,
I will lie down and succumb to this gnawing famine
Hunger overwhelms me,
The moon illuminates the sky,
I will eat of the moon tonight...

>Jim Rodarte

WINTER

Winter is coming, it's on its way,
Soon I will have to get out my sleigh.
Get out my coat, mittens, and hat,
Put away my ball and bat.
Put away my bathing suits,
Go to the store and get snow boots.
Now it is time to go down the hill,
I know my winter will be funfilled.
With glistening snow, and wind blows in my face,
Down the hill I will race.
Make snow angels with great white wings,
It is up to you what winter brings.
Now winter is over, it has been fine,
Spring is arriving, what's on my mind?

Tiffany J. Rose

HAPPINESS

Happiness is gold.
It sounds like a boy's laughter.
It smells like roses in a beautiful meadow.
It tastes like blueberry pie.
It looks like beautiful stars in the night.
It feels like a mother's love.
Happiness feels like the peaceful night.

Jonathan Aaron Saddler
Age: 8

MELISSA GIWER

M onkey
E xcellent
L ove dance
I mprove
S pecial
S uper
A pples

G ymnast
I mportant
W inner
E xciting
R oses

Melissa Giwer
Age: 11

POLAR BEAR

Fuzzy, baby cubs
White, aggressive, cuddly
Protective mothers

Brittany Bates

VOLLEYBALL

V olley the ball.
O ver the net.
L iking the game.
L ooking for spikes.
E veryone plays all the positions.
Y elling encouragement to our team.
B eing the best you can play.
A wesome to play.
L istening to the cheers, when we play well.
L inist after the game, to congratulate the other team.

Meagan Martin
Age: 10

TIC-TAC-TOE -- GI JOE'S

Tic-tac-toe three in a row,
everyone has GI Joe's,
they have little guns,
and you can have fun with GI Joe's.
If you buy GI Joe's you won't be sorry,
If you buy a lot you can have an army.
You can buy them at the store,
and make 'em have a war,
with your little GI Joe's.

Ricky Hackle

CHLOE

One Christmas morning
I woke up to a very happy sight.
There in my mom's arms was my dog,
She held her very tight.

This dog brought joy and love
To our family of three.
My mom, my dad, and me.

After two years we add a brother.
In four more years we have a sister.
Oh how much I really miss her.

She is no longer with us to run and play.
Or go to Grandma's on a Sunday.

This Christmas morning we will be a little sad.
Our dog is not with us and that makes us mad.

She is up in heaven, where the good dogs go.
Down here on earth we miss our dear Chloe.

David Backer
Age: 10

SLOWPOKE

Slowpoke the Pokémon, there he lay.
   He's so lazy he didn't get up all day.
There he is, looks dead as a rock.
   As he sits there on the ocean's dock.
The oceans' waves put him to sleep,
   As he dreams of swimming to the deep.
When he wakes up, he moves away,
   But he'll come back another day.

Andrew Burba
Age: 10

I REMEMBER

I remember Grandpa Lou
Even though I was only a year or two.
I remember his weird black shoes,
I remember him in his chair taking a big snooze.
I remember he would say, "Jakie you're a star."
I know he's with me near or far.
I'll always remember my grandpa Lou,
Sometimes when I think of him, I boohoohoo!

Jacob Robert Pfister
Age: 10

TEACHERS

T eaching
E ducation
A pple
C lassroom
H istory
E ncouraging
R ecess
S weet

> Breana Wright
> Age: 10

TREES

Trees trees they're the center of it all.
Without them there shall not be any oxygen
for us to live,
or for plants to live.
There would be no life.
So when I say the center of it all,
you know what I mean.
Do all life a favor,
take a clue
and stop cutting down trees
plant some more everywhere.

> Allen Teetz II
> Age: 10

TWISTER OF '99

We were asleep in our beds
Early Friday morning,
When a killer tornado
Came without warning.

We took shelter in the basement
Until it could pass.
We heard the roar of the wind,
And the breaking of glass.

When it was safe to come out
We were in for a shock,
To see what the tornado
Had done to our block.

Trees were all down,
Taking fences down too.
But we lost more than that
When the mighty winds blew.

Some of the houses
Were really a sight!
It looked like a giant
Had taken a bite.

Some roofs were missing,
Walls and windows were shattered.
Was everyone all right?
That was really all that mattered.

We checked on our neighbors.
They were safe, to our relief.

Then we looked at the damage
And stared in disbelief.

Emergency crews
Soon arrived on our street,
And the Red Cross offered
People something to eat.

Soon lots of volunteers
Were in our neighborhood,
Helping people save
Anything that they could.

They cut up the trees
And hauled them away.
Then they cleaned up debris,
Working day after day.

We give thanks to God
That we were all right
We know He was with us
On that terrible night.

                                        Ryan Wetterich

Myself
Kind-hearted
Quiet, fun, active
Happy, cheerful, glad, pleasant
Emily

Emily Spotts

OCTOBER

How I've missed October,
A time for chilly winds.
Time for cornstalks, time for pumpkins,
Time for happy grins.

If you look all around you,
What a sight you'll see!
A bunch of kids are all dressed up.
Looks like fun to me!!

Yes, I have missed October,
A wonderful month to me.
But my favorite part, as you've probably guessed,
Is the holiday Halloween!!

Nicole Kathryn Savage
Age: 11

Danielle
Funny,
Loving,
Nice.
Wishes to have a house full of puppies,
Dreams of all people being friends,
Wants to help other people.
Who fears people on the street.
Who is afraid of being alone.
Who believes in herself.
Who loves her family.
Who loves to play baseball.
Who loves to eat pizza.
Who loves her grandma's cookies.
Who plans to be a baseball player.
Who plans to play for the Cincinnati Reds.
Who plans to live a good life.
Whose dreams will come true.

                                Danielle VanDerVelde
                                         Age: 9

Andrew
Fun,
Nice,
Talented.
Wishes to be a baseball player,
Dreams of fantasies,
Wants to get a good education.
Who wonders when I die
What's going to happen to me.
Who is afraid of roller blades.
Who likes sports that aren't boring.
Who believes in God.
Who loves playing baseball.
Who loves video games.
Who loves the snow.
Who plans to have a good life.
Who plans to do well in school.
Who plans to be a good father.
Who loves his family.

Andrew Bryant
Age: 9

CHRISTMAS

C hrist's birthday
H erald angels sing
R udolph the red-nosed reindeer
I cicles falling from trees and roofs
S anta Claus is coming to town
T oy soldiers marching to your house
M istletoe makes people kiss
A ngels singing in the snow
S ongs of joy fill hearts

Brittney Danielle Cornist
Age: 9

IF I WERE A WITCH

If I were a green witch.
I'd make a potion cake.
I'd put frogs and toads in it.
I'd also put snake bones, fingernails
and slime in it.
I'd cook it for two minutes.
Then I would put the icing on it.
Perhaps the icing would have tasted better
if I cooked it.

Sean Griffin
Age: 7

Is it the time I don't want to spend,
That starts to make my family bend?
Bending and breaking apart --
Can I make a fresh new start?
My sister always looks up to me,
I was mean to her, why didn't I see?
For it was myself I was hurting --
By putting her down,
And in exchange for all of her smiles,
I deserve frowns.
I wish I could tell her --
It was all a mistake.
But for all I might say,
Her trust I did break.
That horrid example,
I gave to her all the same,
And by her coping me
I was put to shame.

Elizabeth Shockey
Age: 11

Nature supplies me
Nature gives me food to eat
Nature is real nice

Kris Dawson
Age: 11

SCHOOL

S cience
C lassroom
H istory
Mr. O ldfield
O ffice
L earn

Zachary Lindsey
Age: 11

SPRING

The bright sun shines on
the leaves on the tree all day
while they turn purple.

Katherine Marie Riley
Age: 12

IN MY DREAMS

In my dreams my fantasies come true
Playing in my mind time after time is you
In my dreams we do everything in a pair
Always showing each other how much we care
In my dreams it's only you and me
Being so peaceful and so carefree
In my dreams we're always together
And everything but you blurs by in a mixed color
In my dreams we're endlessly holding hands
You whispering in my ear "I'll always be your man."
In my dreams we're never apart
We are forever safe in one another's heart
In my dreams a nightmare suddenly invades
And us being together quickly fades
In my dreams I have no more fun
The happiness I once had is over and done.

Jenna Ruberg
Age: 12

Coy Whitehead
sleep, awake
fishing, riding, cooking
He helps start the cars.

Coy Whitehead
Age: 8

FRIENDS

Friends are so important,
you don't even know how much.
When there's a death
they're by your side.
When you have a problem
they give a special touch.

Friends are so important,
Even when they're far away.
But really, best friends
are with you, in good and bad,
to stay.

Color never matters,
as long as they care.
Friends will always be near,
they always do their share.

Jami Hugentobler
Age: 12

P ink.
I ts ham tastes good.
G ood pets.
G ood to eat.
Y ou can eat their bacon.

Veronica M. Binder

FRIENDS

Friends are people you can count on
who don't leave you out
or talk behind your back.
When you stumble they keep you going
and when you fall they help you up.

The makeup you use,
the clothes you wear,
or how you do your hair,
doesn't matter to a friend
because they only really care
about what's important.

A friend will always be there,
whether it is a troubled or joyful time.
They don't care what you look like
it's what's inside that they care about.

Kara Lohbeck
Age: 12

Papa
brave, strong
working, playing, driving
He helps me out.

Corey Richards

THE SEASONS

I like all the seasons,
for many reasons.
Summer is hot
and humid.
Fall is not.
It is golden,
red, and brown,
and when I walk
the leaves crunch down.
Winter is cold.
I make a fire,
and drink cocoa.
Spring is windy,
good for a kite.
It soars in flight.
Those are the reasons
I like all the seasons.

Laura Sanman
Age: 11

My pumpkin is big and round,
And it grew on the ground.
It was also bounding on the ground.

Katie Campbell
Age: 8

THE PERFECT FANS

You changed my diapers.
You helped me learn my first steps.
You taught me lessons.
You were always there
When I was crying or when I fell.
You showed me discipline.
I am very grateful for this.
I hope someday that I can be
As great as parents as you are.
I LOVE YOU DADDY AND MARY!!!!!!!!!

Samantha Nicole Rogers
Age: 11

HALLOWEEN

Trick-or-treating black cats
carved pumpkins, scary faces, BOO
leaves falling all around.

Megan Clark

MY PLACE

Birds whistle softly,
Songs of happiness and sorrow.
Rabbits burrow deep in holes,
Waiting for tomorrow.
A weeping willow cries tenderly,
Its tears of morning dew.
Chipmunks yawn, squirrels stretch,
And start the day anew.

On summer days I travel here,
Breathing in the scents,
Of wild flowers and newborn buds,
On trees and by a fence.
Gentle breezes caress my hair,
Like a mother with her child.
The creatures here surround me,
All animals of the wild.

Erin Kay Gillette
Age: 14

Bike
quiet, transport
go, fast, easy
fun, speed, free, adventurous
Ride

Justin Mohr

STEVE YOUNG

My name is Steve Young, my sport is football,
I wasn't very short and I wasn't very tall.

For twenty-five years I had a dream,
To be in the Super Bowl with a great team.

My father, Grit, wanted me to get a job
In the summer,
Instead of sitting around and just getting dumber.

If I didn't have a job I didn't use the car,
But since I had a job I got a chance to travel far.

My parents (Sherry and "Grit")
Wanted to teach me that,
You just can't pull money right out of your hat.

Of course I was a well respected man,
I always had time to sign an autograph for a fan.

Even though I never drank beer,
That helped me to win
The Western Athletic Conference
Player of the year.

First I was drafted by the Express,
But after a couple of years
The USFL turned into a mess.

After the USFL I traveled all the way,
Across the country to Tampa Bay.

The San Francisco 49ers was my next team,
And that's who I'm playing for,
Still following my Super Bowl dream.

Sean Hennessy
Age: 11

WINTERTIME

The bright snow glistens
Children having snowball fights
Christmastime is here.

Corey Gould
Age: 12

Steven
Cool,
Loving,
Athletic.
Wishes to become a baseball player,
Dreams of disappearing,
Wants to become a good athlete.
Who wonders what it would be like to be famous.
Who fears having evil beside them.
Who is afraid of spirits.
Who likes singers.
Who believes in faith.
Who loves baseball.
Who loves fortune tellers.
Who loves sports.
Who loves raisins.
Who plans to be a sports player.
Who plans to take pride in my work.
Who plans to live a good life.
Who wants to become a good athlete.

Steven Burton
Age: 9

Spider sack
small, sticky
hanging, moving, wiggling
growing inside
Spider sack

Lauren Holle

BREAKFAST

I see... The clock says it's time to go downstairs
I hear... Eggs frying on the stove
I smell... Cinnamon rolls baking
I touch... A cool glass of juice
I taste... A juicy red grapefruit
I feel... Full and warm all over
I hear... My mom calling me
I see... It's time to go to school

Julia Catherine Dolan
Age: 10

Moon
whole, bright
shines, reaching, following
cold, happy, scary, shivering
Huge

Jessica Smithson

A GREAT LOSS

I lost a great friend today
A friend who brought me love
Always there for me
Always loving me

This morning when I awoke
I was told he had left me
Tears came rolling down my cheeks
But, those tears were soon replaced with a smile
A smile to hide my truest feelings

I know now my friend is gone for good
I will miss him very much
One day I will see him again
I have to...
I must...
I lost a great friend today

                                              Michael Gwin

                  Snow
               white, ice
          cold, blowing, flurries
         Snow brings me joy.
                 Flakes

                                              Kelly Zeller

IN FANTASY WORLD

Mermaids swim in the crystal-blue sea,
While sailors sing jolly songs with me.
Unicorns prance on the land nearby,
While fairies fly through the bright blue sky.

Pegasus soars over mountain peaks,
Over golden fish in rivers and creeks.
My brother looks up as I read the tales
And smiles as I lead him on fairy tale trails.

Laura E. Grothaus
Age: 7

Wind
cold, hard
blowing, slow, gusty
happy, glad, pleasant, good
Breezy

Laura Grimsley

VETERANS

A veteran is a person who has fought,
In order to achieve what they sought,
All of them fought to the end,
For their country they were to defend,
Some people were on the ground nearly dead,
Others were almost never fed,
So thank the United States veterans.

Justin Scott Forsberg
Age: 12

Colored leaves
pretty, red
holding, falling, flying
high piles
Colored leaves

Kris Wittwer

THE BIG MATCH

Today was the big day
Today the big wrestling match was on.
I didn't care how long it took
I would watch it 'til dawn.

I finished my homework
I took a shower
I went downstairs
and got to work
I turned on the TV
I flipped to channel thirty-three.

I saw the match
all night seeing big people
get in a fight.

I got so hungry
I cooked some popcorn
when I got back
the match was over.

I screamed so loud
my voice was weak
after that I got grounded
for a week.

Keith Andrew Needham
Age: 10

A school is a school
like any other school
You learn arithmetic,
English, and spelling too
You have lunch
with your friends
while your teachers give you tens
And next thing you know
the day ends.

Ta - Seti M. Donald
Age: 11

CHRISTMAS

C aroling
H ome for Christmas
R eindeer
I cicles
S now
T ree
M istletoe
A ngel
S anta Claus

Nick Gehring
Age: 10

BIRDS

Birds fly in the sky
   don't ask me why!
Birds are black, brown, and blue
   just like other animals at the zoo
I like to watch the birds fly by
   up high in the bright blue sky

Shelby Williams
Age: 8

STORM

The trees were swaying in the wind
The lightning was a razor blade
Cutting up the sky
The thunder rolled over the hills
Shaking all in its path.
The rain pelted the ground
Like thousands of bombs
For hours the chaos went on,
Until the sun broke through
The thick gray clouds.

Brandon T. Buschmeier
Age: 13

SPORTS

A thlete,
B aseball,
C atch
D ive,
E nergy,
F oul ball

G ymnastics,
H ome run,
I ce hockey,
J ump,
K ick,

L aps,
M ichael Jordan,
N ine innings,
O ut,
P layer,
Q uarterback,
R ace,

S core,
T ennis,
U mpire,
V iolent,
W ild,
X -ersize,
Y elling,
Z oom.

Danni Scott
Age: 11

FALL

Fall is warm,
and the leaves change colors.
It smells like turkey.
It tastes like pumpkin pie.
It sounds like ghosts crying.
It reminds me of farming.
Fall makes me feel
warm and cozy in my house.

Brad Mummert
Age: 8

Fall is when
The flowers are dying,
The birds are flying south,
Leaves are changing,
Animals are sleeping,

Jena Sweet

Runnin' down the court made a shot
Come back down the court get a block
Sometimes your shot is hot
and sometimes it could be a team leader
and carry the load
You get to play "D"
so you can hit a three.
Sometimes you play
and sometimes you ride the bench
as long as it is a play-off benth you clinch.

DeAndre Cheatham
Age: 11

BEING A LEFTY

Life is very hard for me,
Than lots of other people.
Sometimes I look awkward,
Sometimes my handwriting isn't very good.
But, I try very hard,
Harder than most.
Because you see I'm a lefty!

Tim O'Sullivan
Age: 11